MAKING MONEY ONLINE: BOOK 4

BY MICHAEL CALLUM MAYAKA

CONTENT CREATION AND MONETIZATION

FOREWORD:

In today's digital age, making money online has become a viable and accessible option for individuals seeking financial independence or additional income streams. The internet offers a plethora of opportunities that allow you to leverage your skills, creativity, and resources to generate revenue. This guide aims to provide you with valuable insights, strategies, and practical tips on how to make money online effectively.

This book is part of a series for more information see Further reading at the end of this book.

Table of Contents

Foreword: 3

4. Content Creation and Monetization 6

    4.1 Starting a Blog or Website: A Gateway to Online Success 7

        1. Define Your Purpose and Target Audience: 8

        2. Choose a Domain Name and Web Hosting: 8

        3. Select a Content Management System (CMS): 9

        4. Design and Customize Your Website: 10

        5. Craft Compelling Content: 11

        6. Implement SEO Strategies: 11

        7. Engage with Your Audience: 12

        8. Monetize Your Blog: 13

        9. Analyze and Improve: 13

        Conclusion: 14

    4.2 Video Content Creation on YouTube 15

        1. Finding Your Niche: 16

        2. Planning and Creating Engaging Videos: 16

        3. Search Engine Optimization (SEO): 18

        4. Consistency and Frequency: 18

        5. Building an Engaged Community: 19

        6. Monetizing Your Channel: 20

        Conclusion: 21

    4.3 Podcasting and Audio Content: Tapping into the Power of Audio 23

        Creating Compelling Podcasts: 24

        Monetizing Your Audio Content: 26

        Promoting Your Podcast: 28

        Conclusion: 30

4.4 Social Media and Influencer Marketing: Harnessing the Power of Online Influence 31

    Here are some key benefits of social media and influencer marketing: 33

    To leverage social media and influencer marketing effectively, consider the following tips: 35

Further reading: 39

4. CONTENT CREATION AND MONETIZATION

4.1 STARTING A BLOG OR WEBSITE: A GATEWAY TO ONLINE SUCCESS

In the digital era, starting a blog or website has become an increasingly popular way to share ideas, provide valuable content, and even generate income. Whether you have a passion for writing, expertise in a specific niche, or a desire to showcase your creativity, launching a blog or website can open doors to numerous opportunities. This section will guide you through the essential steps to kickstart your online presence and establish a successful blog or website.

1. DEFINE YOUR PURPOSE AND TARGET AUDIENCE:

Before diving into the technical aspects, it's crucial to define your blog's purpose and identify your target audience. Are you planning to share your personal experiences, offer advice in a particular field, or promote a business? Understanding your objectives will help shape your content strategy and create a focused and engaging blog.

2. CHOOSE A DOMAIN NAME AND WEB HOSTING:

Selecting a domain name is an important step in establishing your online identity. It should be concise, memorable, and relevant to your blog's theme. Once you've decided on a domain name, you'll need to choose a reliable web hosting service. Compare different hosting providers to find one that offers good uptime, security features, scalability, and customer support.

3. SELECT A CONTENT MANAGEMENT SYSTEM (CMS):

A content management system simplifies the process of creating and managing your blog or website. The most popular CMS is WordPress, known for its user-friendly interface, extensive customization options, and vast plugin library. Alternatively, you can explore other CMS platforms like

Joomla or Drupal, depending on your specific needs.

4. DESIGN AND CUSTOMIZE YOUR WEBSITE:

The design and layout of your blog or website play a crucial role in attracting and retaining visitors. Select a visually appealing theme that aligns with your brand and provides a pleasant user experience. Customize the colours, fonts, and overall appearance to create a unique and professional look. Ensure your site is mobile-friendly, as an increasing number of users access the internet through their smartphones.

5. CRAFT COMPELLING CONTENT:

Content is the backbone of any successful blog or website. Develop a content strategy that focuses on delivering valuable, informative, and engaging articles, blog posts, or multimedia content. Conduct thorough research, use credible sources, and infuse your unique voice into your writing. Consistency is key, so establish a regular posting schedule to keep your audience engaged.

6. IMPLEMENT SEO STRATEGIES:

Search Engine Optimization (SEO) helps improve your blog's visibility in search engine results and attracts organic traffic. Optimize your content by incorporating relevant keywords, writing descriptive meta tags, and using header tags. Build quality backlinks from reputable websites and ensure your site loads quickly for optimal user experience.

7. ENGAGE WITH YOUR AUDIENCE:

Building a loyal readership requires active engagement with your audience. Respond to comments, encourage discussions, and foster a sense of community. Utilize social media platforms to promote your content and connect with your audience. Engaging with your readers helps establish trust, loyalty, and a stronger online presence.

8. MONETIZE YOUR BLOG:

If your goal is to monetize your blog, explore various revenue streams. You can display relevant advertisements through platforms like Google AdSense, join affiliate marketing programs, offer sponsored content, or create and sell your own products or services. It's essential to strike a balance between monetization and providing value to your audience to maintain their trust.

9. ANALYZE AND IMPROVE:

Regularly analyze your blog's performance using analytics tools like Google Analytics. Track your visitors, page views, bounce rate, and engagement metrics to identify areas for improvement. Use the insights gained to refine your content strategy, improve user experience, and grow your blog's reach.

CONCLUSION:

Starting a blog or website is an exciting journey that allows you to share your passion, knowledge, and creativity with the world. By following the steps outlined above, you can establish a compelling online presence, connect with your target audience, and potentially generate income. Remember to stay consistent, adapt to feedback, and continuously improve your content and user experience to ensure long-term success in the competitive online landscape.

4.2 VIDEO CONTENT CREATION ON YOUTUBE

YouTube has emerged as one of the most popular platforms for content creators to share their videos and connect with millions of viewers worldwide. With its vast user base and monetization options, YouTube provides an excellent opportunity for individuals to make money online through video content creation. This section will explore the essentials of creating compelling videos on YouTube and monetizing your channel effectively.

1. FINDING YOUR NICHE:

To succeed on YouTube, it's crucial to identify your niche or area of expertise. Determine the topics you are passionate about or possess knowledge in. This will help you create content that resonates with your target audience and establishes you as an authority in your chosen niche.

2. PLANNING AND CREATING ENGAGING VIDEOS:

a. Content Strategy: Develop a content strategy that aligns with your niche and audience's interests. Plan your video topics, titles, and formats in advance to maintain consistency and keep your viewers engaged.

b. Quality Production: Invest in good equipment, such as cameras, microphones, and lighting, to ensure high-quality videos. Focus on clear audio, proper lighting, and visually appealing visuals to enhance the viewing experience.

c. Storytelling and Scripting: Craft a compelling narrative or story for your videos. Plan your scripts, transitions, and visuals to create a captivating flow. Hook your viewers from the beginning and maintain their interest throughout the video.

d. Editing: Learn basic video editing skills or use editing software to enhance your videos. Edit out any unnecessary segments, add visual effects, transitions, and background music to create a polished final product.

3. SEARCH ENGINE OPTIMIZATION (SEO):

Optimize your video titles, descriptions, and tags with relevant keywords to improve your videos' visibility in YouTube's search results. Conduct keyword research to identify popular and relevant search terms that can attract more viewers to your channel.

4. CONSISTENCY AND FREQUENCY:

Consistency is key on YouTube. Develop a posting schedule and stick to it. Regularly upload new videos to keep your audience engaged and attract new subscribers. Consider the ideal frequency of video uploads based on your niche and audience preferences.

5. BUILDING AN ENGAGED COMMUNITY:

Engage with your viewers by responding to comments, asking for feedback, and encouraging them to subscribe and share your videos. Create a sense of community by interacting with your audience through live streams, Q&A sessions, or collaborations with other YouTubers in your niche.

6. MONETIZING YOUR CHANNEL:

YouTube offers various monetization options for eligible channels. To start earning money from your videos, consider the following methods:

a. Ad Revenue: Enable monetization on your channel and allow YouTube to display ads on your videos. You earn a share of the ad revenue generated from your content.

b. Sponsorships and Brand Deals: Collaborate with brands or companies that align with your content and negotiate sponsored videos or brand partnerships.

c. Merchandise and Merch Shelf: Create and sell your merchandise, such as t-shirts, mugs, or accessories, to your loyal fanbase.

Utilize the Merch Shelf feature to promote and sell your products directly on your YouTube channel.

d. Channel Memberships: Offer exclusive perks and content to your most dedicated fans by setting up a channel membership program. Subscribers pay a monthly fee to access these exclusive benefits.

e. Crowdfunding: Use platforms like Patreon or Ko-fi to allow your viewers to support your channel through voluntary donations.

CONCLUSION:

Video content creation on YouTube presents an exciting opportunity to share your passion, expertise, and creativity while making money online. By finding your niche, planning and creating engaging videos, optimizing for search, building a community, and monetizing your channel strategically, you can turn your YouTube presence into a sustainable income stream. Remember, building a successful YouTube channel takes time, effort, and consistent dedication, so stay persistent and continue learning from your audience's feedback to refine and improve your content over time.

4.3 PODCASTING AND AUDIO CONTENT: TAPPING INTO THE POWER OF AUDIO

In recent years, podcasting has experienced an explosion in popularity, becoming a prominent form of audio content consumed by millions of people worldwide. With its accessibility and versatility, podcasting offers an excellent opportunity for individuals to share their knowledge, stories, and creativity while also monetizing their content. This section will explore the world of podcasting and provide insights on how to create and monetize audio content effectively.

CREATING COMPELLING PODCASTS:

1. Identifying Your Niche: Choose a specific topic or theme for your podcast that aligns with your interests, expertise, and target audience. This helps to differentiate your content in a crowded podcasting landscape.

2. Planning and Structure: Develop a format for your podcast, including episode length, segments, and a consistent release schedule. Planning ahead ensures a smooth and organized flow of content.

3. Quality Recording and Production: Invest in a decent microphone and audio editing

software to ensure high-quality sound. Clear and professional audio enhances the listening experience and reflects positively on your brand.

4. Engaging Content: Focus on creating informative, entertaining, or thought-provoking episodes that resonate with your audience. Engage listeners through storytelling, interviews with experts, or discussions on relevant topics.

5. Showcasing Personality: Infuse your podcast with your unique personality and style. Authenticity helps build a connection with your audience and keeps them coming back for more.

MONETIZING YOUR AUDIO CONTENT:

1. Sponsorships and Advertisements: Once your podcast gains traction and attracts a significant audience, you can explore sponsorships and advertising opportunities. Collaborate with relevant brands or platforms that align with your podcast's niche.

2. Crowdfunding and Donations: Offer your listeners the option to support your podcast through crowdfunding platforms or direct donations. Engage with your audience and provide exclusive perks or bonus content as incentives for their support.

3. Merchandise and Product Sales: Create branded merchandise or products related to your podcast. This can include t-shirts, mugs, or books. Promote and sell these items to your audience as a way to generate additional income.

4. Paid Memberships and Subscriptions: Offer premium or exclusive content to subscribers who pay a monthly or yearly fee. This can include bonus episodes, early access to content, or behind-the-scenes insights.

5. Live Events and Workshops: Organize live events, workshops, or webinars related to your podcast's topic. Charge admission

fees or offer premium tickets to monetize your expertise and provide value to your audience in a more interactive setting.

6. Affiliate Marketing: Recommend products or services that align with your podcast's theme and become an affiliate partner. Earn a commission for each sale or sign-up generated through your affiliate links.

PROMOTING YOUR PODCAST:

1. Effective Podcast Titles and Descriptions: Craft compelling titles and descriptions that accurately represent your podcast's content. Optimize them with

relevant keywords to improve discoverability on podcast platforms.

2. Social Media Promotion: Leverage social media platforms to engage with your audience, share episode highlights, behind-the-scenes insights, and encourage listeners to subscribe and leave reviews.

3. Collaboration and Cross-Promotion: Collaborate with other podcasters or influencers in your niche. Guest appearances on their podcasts or featuring them on your show can expand your reach and attract new listeners.

4. Utilizing Email Marketing: Build an email list and regularly communicate with your

subscribers. Send updates, exclusive content, and promotional offers to keep them engaged and informed.

CONCLUSION:

Podcasting provides an exciting avenue for individuals to create and share audio content with a global audience. By focusing on creating engaging episodes, implementing effective monetization strategies, and promoting your podcast strategically, you can turn your passion for audio content into a profitable venture. Embrace the power of podcasting and discover the endless possibilities for connecting with listeners, sharing knowledge, and monetizing your creativity.

4.4 SOCIAL MEDIA AND INFLUENCER MARKETING: HARNESSING THE POWER OF ONLINE INFLUENCE

In recent years, social media has revolutionized the way we connect, communicate, and consume information. It has also become a powerful platform for businesses to reach their target audience and promote their products or services. One of the most effective strategies within social media marketing is influencer marketing.

This approach leverages the reach and influence of popular social media personalities, known as influencers, to endorse and promote brands. In this article, we will explore the concept of social media and influencer marketing, its benefits, and how to leverage this strategy effectively.

Social media platforms such as Instagram, YouTube, TikTok, and Twitter have given rise to a new breed of online celebrities who have amassed a significant following. These influencers have built a loyal fan base by creating engaging content that resonates with their audience. They have established themselves as trusted authorities and trendsetters in various niches, including beauty, fashion, fitness, travel, and more.

HERE ARE SOME KEY BENEFITS OF SOCIAL MEDIA AND INFLUENCER MARKETING:

1. Expanded Reach and Targeted Audience: Influencers have a dedicated following that aligns with their interests and demographics. Partnering with influencers allows businesses to tap into their existing audience, expanding their reach and connecting with potential customers who may have otherwise been difficult to reach through traditional marketing methods.

2. Enhanced Credibility and Trust: Influencers have built trust and credibility

with their followers over time. When they endorse a product or service, their audience tends to view it as a genuine recommendation rather than a traditional advertisement. This trust factor can significantly impact purchasing decisions and brand perception.

3. Authentic and Engaging Content: Influencers are known for their ability to create authentic, relatable, and engaging content. By collaborating with influencers, brands can leverage their creativity and storytelling skills to create compelling campaigns that resonate with the target audience. This helps build brand awareness and fosters a deeper connection with potential customers.

TO LEVERAGE SOCIAL MEDIA AND INFLUENCER MARKETING EFFECTIVELY, CONSIDER THE FOLLOWING TIPS:

1. Define Your Goals and Target Audience: Clearly define your marketing objectives and identify the target audience you want to reach. Research influencers who align with your brand values, niche, and target demographics.

2. Build Relationships: Take the time to build genuine relationships with influencers. Engage with their content, provide value,

and show interest in their work. This helps establish a rapport and increases the chances of successful collaborations in the future.

3. Collaborate Strategically: Work with influencers who align with your brand image and target audience. Discuss campaign objectives, deliverables, and expectations upfront. Co-create content that seamlessly integrates your brand message without appearing overly promotional.

4. Track and Measure Results: Use analytics tools to track the performance and effectiveness of your influencer marketing campaigns. Monitor metrics such as engagement, reach, conversions, and ROI.

Adjust your strategies based on the insights gained to optimize future campaigns.

5. Stay Compliant and Transparent: Adhere to the guidelines and regulations set by the respective social media platforms and advertising standards. Ensure that sponsored content is clearly disclosed to maintain transparency and build trust with the audience.

In conclusion, social media and influencer marketing offer immense potential for businesses to connect with their target audience in a more authentic and impactful way. By leveraging the influence of social media personalities, brands can expand their reach, enhance credibility, and create engaging content that drives conversions. However, it's crucial to approach influencer marketing strategically, aligning with the right influencers and maintaining transparency to achieve the best results.

FURTHER READING:

If you enjoyed this book, please consider reading one of the other books in the series:

Making Money Online: Book 1 (Understanding the Online Landscape)

Making Money Online: Book 2 (E-commerce and Online Retail)

Making Money Online: Book 3 (Freelancing and Remote Work)

Making Money Online: Book 4 (Content Creation and Monetization)

Making Money Online: Book 5 (Online Tutoring and Education)

Making Money Online: Book 6 (Online Surveys, Microtasks, and Rewards)

Making Money Online: Book 7 (Online Investments and Trading)

Making Money Online: Book 8 (Creating and Selling Digital Assets)

Making Money Online: Book 9 (Online Consulting and Coaching)

Making Money Online: Book 10 (Maximizing Online Income Opportunities)

All the books can be found on Amazon as Kindle and Paperback, or you can buy the complete edition which contains the full series in one book. The complete edition is available as Kindle, Paperback and exclusively as Hardback. You can find all the links in my book site: books.michaelmayaka.co.uk.

www.ingramcontent.com/pod-product-compliance
Lightning Source LLC
Chambersburg PA
CBHW040254220526
45473CB00001B/477